"....I just finished SKY BLUE. I found
pain, caring , and though
It was interesting the way that the e
each new ha

Bruce Glasser is a writer and artist. His work has appeared on several television programs including the BBC and ITV. Articles about him have been published in, "The Guardian," "The Daily Telegraph," and, "The Brit Art Directory." The Victoria and Albert museum have archived information about his paintings.

bruceglasser.com

Some of the haiku has been previously published in COURAGE a collection of Bruce Glasser's poetry.

THIS BOOK IS DEDICATED TO:
MY PRECIOUS FAMILY

glasserbruce@gmail.com
bruceglasser.com

cover design: Bruce Glasser

SKY BLUE

HAIKU

BRUCE GLASSER

TABLE OF CONTENTS

GOOD - 93 CONTROL - 94 SOMEWHERE - 95 SHOCK - 96 RIVER - 97
DEMONS - 98 WRITE - 99 PASSAGE - 100 BRILLIANT - 101 MOVE - 102
SHY - 103 TIME - 104 LIGHT - 105 KISS - 106 JOKE - 107 FALL -108
SEE - 109 SWEET - 110 PETALS - 111 HEALTH - 112 SONG -113 CAN - 114
THUNDER - 115 BARK - 116 FEEL - 117 RAGE - 118 KING - 119 OCEAN - 120
CHEAT - 121 FREE - 122 SUN - 123 LAND - 124 PATTERNS - 125 FLOW - 126
LOVE - 127 CARE - 128 HEAT - 129 CENTRE - 130 HOW - 131 SEE - 132
TAKE - 133 QUICK - 134 RUN - 135 DAY - 136 FREE - 137 HELP - 138
WHY - 139 WHEN - 140 GIVE - 141 STAY - 142 STOP - 143 TREAT - 144
TAKEN - 145 FIND - 146 CARE - 147 - CHANGES - 148 HOME - 149
PROTECT - 150 PLACE - 151 HEAVEN - 152 PATH - 153 EARTH - 154
LEAVE - 155 FIELD - 156 IMAGE - 157 POETRY - 158 SILENCE - 159
WHEN - 160 MUSIC - 161 WHITE - 162 MIND - 163 DISTURB - 164 RUSH - 165
SHAPE - 166 CINEMA - 167 NOISE - 168 BRUSH - 169 DEEP - 170
ALONE - 171 STAY - 172 DREAM - 173 VENOM - 174 WHAT - 175 NAKED - 176
ROOM - 177 COLD - 178 STEADY - 179 FRESH - 180 NEWS - 181
DESPERATE - 182 BIG - 183 REMEMBER - 184 CORNER - 185 NOTHING - 186
ANGEL - 187 HARMONY - 188 APRIL - 189 FINISH - 190 SORRY - 191
GROUCH - 192 COME - 193 LONGING - 194 STRUGGLE - 195 WINTER - 196
FOREST - 197 DEEP - 198 TIME - 199 TRY - 200 BLUE - 201 SOD - 202

FALLING - 203 SEASON - 204 DRIVE - 205 FEAR - 206 MAKE - 207
APPLE - 208 MINIMUM - 209 POINT - 210 NORMAL - 211 FLUSHED - 212
DAY - 213 MAGIC - 214 TREASURE - 215 NATURE - 216 HORIZON - 217
SIMPLE - 218 COURAGE - 219 WONDER - 220 REACH - 221 SHADOWS - 222
FREE - 223 SPIRIT - 224 TEARS - 225 FALL - 226 WHY - 227 LIGHT - 228
STRIKE - 229 CAREFUL - 230 DROP - 231 STONES -232 SHARP - 233
SUNRISE - 234 EASY - 235 AMAZING - 236 NEW - 237 MOUNTAIN - 238
MEADOW - 239 LOVE - 240 LIFE - 241 WINDOW - 242 GOOD - 243
DESTINY - 244 ANCIENT - 245 PAPER - 246 ICE - 247 SAND - 248
CRACK - 249 TEAR - 250 LOST - 251SIMPLE - 252 TICKET - 253
HUMAN - 254 ONLY - 255 PALE - 256 HOPE - 257 COMEDY - 258 WAIT - 259
FOREVER - 260 SAD - 261 AGE - 262 EXCUSE - 263 TREASURE - 264
FREEDOM - 265 PERSON - 266 ESCAPE - 267 HAT - 268 STRAWBERRY - 269
HARD - 270 WELL - 271 HANG - 272 LILLY - 273 OCEAN - 274 DOG TOY - 275
SPRING - 276 STEEL - 277 KING - 278 SHARP - 279 HARBOUR - 280
STORM - 281 EDGE - 282 FIRE - 283 SPRING - 284 BYGONE - 285
WISE - 286 ELECTRIC - 287 BROKEN - 288 ODD - 289 PALACE - 290
BLACK - 291 LEAF - 292 BOLD - 293 SHADOWS - 294 BLUE - 295
WAKE - 296 FREEDOM - 297 FLY - 298 BUD - 299 ROSE - 300

SKY BLUE

She stood in her sky
Blue dress in the green meadow
The blue sky above her

TRUTH

What truth is out there
That shines an intense light on
What is so wrong

FEELING

Tell me what you are
Feeling so I can shed a tear
For your broken dreams

ROMANTIC

So beautiful it makes
Life roar with the sharp colours
Of a thousand rainbows

WHAT

What will you say when
The sun falls beneath the edge
Of our vivid world

JOKE

Please do not use
My foolish acts of kindness
As some kind of joke

WINTER

Deep in winter's grip
I feel your unbridled warmth
And cherish the fire

NAKED

The naked truth that
Feels so hard that it will scratch
Like an old lion's claws

DROP

A drop of new rain
Sitting on a red flower
Reflecting the sun

CLOSE

We must not close
The pathways that lead us to
Places of wonder

END

A dead end that we
All travel to strutting on
With a vacant smile

DEPRESSION

Depression you are
So cruel that I spit on your
Face with acid words

REMEMBER

Remember those times
When life felt like a miracle
To be cherished

SAD

Why be oh so sad
When your garden is so full
Of delicious fruit

CLOSE

How close can you be
To the hard truth that you can
Feel with your cold heart

FIRST

Be first with the words
That send you to fresh new shores
Sun drenched beaches

STAR

Stars shine oh so far
Back in aeons of galactic
Time to show your light

DAY

No day that starts with
Thunder's peril is free from
Life's reality

PASS

Pass through the path
That twists and turns making it
Hard to keep your love

WHY

Why should you not think
That being free is your goal
To be in the sun

TREE

Be sturdy my tree
That moans in the harsh cold wind
Make leaves in the spring

WALK

Walk slow and be free
To wonder at the beauty
In the path of life

BEE

Bee fly straight and true
To the large yellow flower
So full of pollen

MISS

Do not miss kind acts
That are meant to make your life
Just that bit better

WHY

Why crush your new dreams
With sorrow that stops your life
With fences of stone

WINGS

Wings rush in the sky
A flock of frantic black birds
Seeking hard branches

DO NOT

Do not tell me that
You have lost the way to my
Warm and full heart

DEVIL

The devil looked
At me and broke into a wide
Rotten teeth smile

DISTANCE

The distance between
Us is a valley full of
Thorn covered trees

TEARS

What tears are these that
Run down your reddened cheeks
Oh such sad sorrow

ART

I lost the painting
I made of the sun breaking
Through heavy dark clouds

NEW

What new feeling is
This that turns our precious
Days into wonder

WHEN

Will we see the truth
So dear that it melts our hearts
Into golden dreams

SEA

The sea oh so rough
Making our voyage so hard
That we cannot stand

NEVER

Never do that thing
That silences the new day
Into a long night

MASKS

These African masks
So rich in stories they can
Tell of beasts and men

IF

If only there is a
Way of ending this chronic
Pain without hard drugs

JOURNEY

We walk together
Seeing the refreshing wind
Play with her silk scarf

TREE

Every day I watch my
Tree becoming full with the
Good forces of spring

FREE

It would be so good
If we could clear away the
Hurt - to be so free

SWIM

Swim my friend to the
Shore that beckons your presence
With round golden stones

COURAGE

Be good to me my
Courage to see the new light
Of being so strong

LIGHT

See the light that shines
Oh so bright on the new stars
Of our fertile love

FLY

Little fly in our
Car riding with us to a
Farm full of more flies

LEAVES

The rich and so deep
Coloured leaves that grace our
Trees with blooming life

BANDAGE

Take this bandage off
My wound to cover my cuts
With soothing lotions

FREE

Be free to roam this
Land full of fresh naked dreams
That take you so high

NIGHT

These nights so full of
Dreams that take me so very
Far into new lands

DAY

What day is this that
Starts with a blast of cold air
That quickens our hearts

BEASTS

What beasts are these that
Take my mind into unwanted
Places that are haunted

PEACE

The wind rolled free
Through the valley of flowers
To spread their rich seeds

SCENT

To smell the new scent
Of a flower just hand picked
Is our paradise

USELESS

Do not tell me that
I write words that are useless
Just open your mind

COVER

Cover me with warm
Quilts with patches of colours
So rich in odd shapes

BLUE

Sky so blue over
The desert sands that it flows
For all infinity

WATER

Water running so
Fast that it blurs the ways to
The churning sea's roar

LAND

This land that fills the
Eye with the spirit of life
Is forever green

BURN

Do not burn your way
To a place that troubles your
Spirit or your love

DEEP

Deep within your thoughts
Is a place so warm and full
Of life's silver dreams

MONSTER

Stop monster of doubt
That wrecks the days of reason
And fills us with dread

KING

The King on his throne
Turned towards his jester
To break his dark thoughts

FANTASY

What fantasy is this
That is rich in image and spirit
That travels so far

SAY

How can you say you
Are the only one who can see
The path to true love

LEAF

Flowing down the stream
A single red leaf fallen from
A tree this autumn

GOLD

Clothed in rich gold
Oh so bright that it feels she
Is wearing armour

POWER

To feel the power that
Surges through the canyon walls
Swim against the stream

SUMMER

Feel the summer heat
So warm that it draws the sweat
From my naked skin

NOTHING

Nothing can make me
Feel so down when I hear words
Said without any truth

CLOUD

A large cloud so
Dark that it heralds hard rain
That will fill the stream

END

A new end to what
Was getting to be a pain
Is oh so welcome

NEVER

Never do that thing
That silences the new day
Into a long night

THE SAME

If it is always
The same I would throw it as
Far as I can see

MASTER

The master told me
To let the winds of life flow
In deeper circles

THINGS

What things are now there
That give me what I wanted
To nourish our joy

HARD

It is so really
Hard to face the unwanted
Words made of bad lies

WEAK

I feel weak in the face
Of time that runs away with
My precious new days

WONDERS

Wonders oh so deep
That they crack the ice cold shield
That covers darkness

SATISFACTION

What satisfaction
Do we get when we make a
Work of art so grand

PARADISE

If only we knew the
Way to a paradise to
Feed our bankrupt souls

SMOOTH

Be oh so smooth that
All the hard rough edges are now
So brilliant to touch

RACE

Race so fast tearing
Up the track with the power
Of the machine's speed

FRESH

These new ideas are so
Fresh that it stuns the course of
Life's many directions

THE DAY

The day started like
A lion waiting to feed on
Blood soaked prey

SURE

It would be so good
To be sure of our path in
Life's odd, funny ways

THE BIRD

Take flight into wind
So strong that it tips your wings
In such awkward ways

SHIP

The ship cutting the
Waves and splitting the dark sea
With the port in sight

WIND

Winds so strong blowing
Ever stronger joined by rolls
Of thunder and rain

RIVER

River run quick and hard
To join the vast sea to join
The churning tall waves

DUTY

It is my duty
To tell you the truth even
If it strikes a nerve

MISSING

You are missing a
Feeling that alters the way
You see our new world

FRAIL

How frail we feel
When our lives take a wrong turn
It is oh so hard

RESPITE

I feel sorry that I
Have been such a bother that
I will need to go

GOOD

What good will it do
To see the error of my
Funny foolish ways

CONTROL

I do not want to
Control the way you see your
Cold and frozen world

SOMEWHERE

Somewhere there is a
Place oh so beautiful that
No person has seen

SHOCK

The shock ran through his
Mind that it shook him to his
Core to blind his love

RIVER

Diving in to swim
Through the raging rapids of
Water bashing stones

DEMONS

Make the rain fall so
Hard that it washes demons
From my frantic life

WRITE

Write those words of hurt
That fester in your sad heart
To make such hard tears

PASSAGE

You know the way to
Valleys so far from our home
So full of flowers

BRILLIANT

Be oh so brilliant
That those who are around you
Are feeling stunned

MOVE

Move oh so fast that
The wind cannot catch the spirit
Of your life's true force

SHY

You held back being
So shy that your face betrayed
Your feelings of fear

TIME

The passage of time
That teaches us new lessons
In the way we are

LIGHT

The light oh so bright
The colours so full, so vibrant
A quilt made of song

KISS

Your kiss oh so sweet
That it sings of our true hearts
Beating out our love

JOKE

There are to many hard
Jokes that are told with such bad
Intentions and sneers

FALL

Do not fall so far
That the way up is filled
With sharp jagged stones

SEE

Try to see that your
Love gives me all I want to
Power our real love

SWEET

Oh how so sweet it
Is to see in the new day's
Light so warm and bright

PETALS

Cherry petals oh
So pink cover the wet ground
Soon decay to soil

HEALTH

So good it is to
Wake to start the fresh new day
So full of energy

SONG

The bird sings his song
Waiting so keenly for a
An answer in song

CAN

I try the best I
Can to not miss the wonder
That still surrounds me

THUNDER

Lightening and rumbles
Flashing through the deep darkness
Of the midnight sky

BARK

I did not know that
Our small white hair dog could bark
So loud to scare us

FEEL

Feel the wind so fresh
That it turns my weather worn
Hands red and so cold

RAGE

What rage is this that
Makes his spirit fight with such
An awesome power

KING

The King looked down
To see his jester's funny
Fall that made him laugh

OCEAN

Ocean use your waves
To wash clean the scars that men
Make on your sand beach

CHEAT

He will not cheat you
Out of what you think is good
I will be your guard

FREE

So good to feel free
Free to make the day do what
You always wanted

SUN

Burn our bright sun send
Your burning light to planets
Caught in frozen space

LAND

This land full of rocks
So large that they form mountains
Holding back the sea

PATTERNS

How theses colours that
Fill the patterns on an old quilt
Make my bedtime sing

FLOW

Flow ever faster my
River of dreams that fill my
Nights with stark visions

LOVE

Love be so kind that
Every day you grow richer
And full of kind thoughts

CARE

I care that you care
We care together for those
That need our kindness

HEAT

Do not let the heat
Of the moment grow into
Something we regret

CENTRE

At the centre of our
Lives the tree of life grows so
Full of rich, ripe fruit

HOW

I now know how the
Beating of our hearts flows in
Ever increasing rhythms

SEE

If only we could see
That first precious moment when
The sun brings new light

TAKE

To take from the field
A rich harvest of firm fruit
A welcome reward

QUICK

They were quick to see
How are warmth dissipated
A volley of sneers

RUN

Run fast, run free to
Get the wind flowing around
Your naked limbs

DAY

The day broke on the
Horizon with a clarity of
Light that stunned the eye

FREE

When we are free to
Be true to ourselves it will
Be our salvation

HELP

She tried to help her
Son to see through his hard pain
To see tears flowing

WHY

Why do the branches
Bend at such awkward angles
To catch the sunlight

WHEN

The day's searing heat
The cold night comes to cool the
Day's burning hot wind

GIVE

I want to give you
The key to my lonely life
Please be so careful

STAY

Stay little bird to sing
Your sweet songs that fill my heart
With such endless joy

STOP

Stop shouting your ideas
That only make sense to your mind
That is full of hurt

TREAT

It is such a treat
To see the smile spread across
Your once too sad face

TAKEN

It was taken from me
With just some bad and bent words
I will now strike back

FIND

What will we find for
Our love that will give it that
Bolt of electricity

CARE

For those who do not
Care for the dignity of life
Do not come near me

CHANGES

Bring in the new flow
In the patterns of grey clouds
That turns them to rain

HOME

How good it is to
Feel the warmth of being
At home - fire burning

PROTECT

My hands are covered
In a warm cloth to hold a
Bird fallen from nest

PLACE

What place is this that
Feels oh so right that I fall
Under its rich spell

HEAVEN

My heaven is dark
To all those that cannot see
The meaning of me

PATH

The path through the woods
Is filled with bright blue flowers
A scent oh so strong

EARTH

The dark black, rich earth
With the nourishing power
For fruit, flowers, trees

LEAVE

She did want to leave
She knew her sadness will not
Heal such bad feelings

FIELD

A field full of bright
Yellow flowers to become
Oil from the rape seed

IMAGE

The image sticks in the
Mind so powerful that I
Never will be free

POETRY

What words are these that
Speak to a beautiful truth
Poetry so profound

SILENCE

The silence was deep
So deep that not a single sound
Could escape our love

WHEN

When will the bare trees
Force their leaves to the sunlight
To make rich fruit

MUSIC

The music flows when
The rhythm of the stars sings
The songs of new life

WHITE

Does it have to be
So white that just to look at
It hurts our old eyes

MIND

Our minds meet in ways
That are so beautiful that
We can embrace love

DISTURB

Do not disturb the
Way the light plays on the floor
It is something special

RUSH

Please do not rush out
The door we can still talk to
Find a better way

SHAPE

It will not take shape
If the desire to make a work
Of art is so dull

CINEMA

The cinema is
Closed our dreams are left on
An old blank white screen

NOISE

The noise is ever
Louder as the lightening
Strikes near our home

BRUSH

The artist's brush so
Full of dried colourful paint
Waiting to be clean

DEEP

Fall ever so deep in
The ocean of life's harmony to
Be full of wonder

ALONE

How different is
The distance between being
Alone and solitude

STAY

Should you want to stay
It would be nice if you could
Bring us fresh flowers

DREAM

To dream the dreams that
Flow from the rivers of my soul
Be light of distant stars

VENOM

Your words have the venom
That spits on the sadness that
Breaks the hard new day

WHAT

What river is this that
Rushes through this parched land
To carve the canyon walls

NAKED

The naked light bulb
That sends its brash light to reach
The place darkness dwells

ROOM

The room is empty
Only one window's curtain
A sliver of light

COLD

Her cold frozen stare
Spoke of nightmares that haunted
Her hard twisted face

STEADY

Be steady, retain
Your fine balance take your days
Searching for her love

FRESH

How fresh it is to
Feel the cool wind circling your
Fresh naked pink skin

NEWS

Bring on the good news
That will give new life to old,
Forgotten, stale, ideas

DESPERATE

Why be desperate
When you have plenty of time
To plant seeds of love

BIG

It looked to be
Too big to cover the deep
Hole in your soul

REMEMBER

Just remember when
Your unending smiles gave you
The happiest of days

CORNER

The dark corner of
The room has a mystery of
Unending power

NOTHING

There is nothing you
Can say that will take the hurt
Away from my heart

ANGEL

The angel sat on my
Lap telling me stories so
Funny - I wet myself

HARMONY

The harmony of the
Songs of life at my front door
I am so silent

APRIL

Each April spring rushes
To bring flowers to set for
Fruit for our garden

FINISH

If only we could
Finish what we started we
Could relax tonight

SORRY

I wish I did not
Regret having lost so many
Times we cherished

GROUCH

The grouch who could not
See any thing to be happy
Blindly fell in love

COME

Come with me to walk
Among the heaven sent stars
That light our true way

LONGING

I am longing for
The spirit of feelings that
Brings new riots of joy

STRUGGLE

Why struggle with those
Memories that have lost their
Ways that hurt just you

WINTER

The brilliant white snow
So fresh, so clean, so cold, so
Full of winter's breath

FOREST

The light is fading
In the deep now dark forest
Trees just an outline

DEEP

How deep can we go
Into the canyons of dark
That circles our old souls

TIME

I recall the times
When we ran down the garden
Chasing the bouncing ball

TRY

I would like to try
Something that is really new
That is so awesome

BLUE

The inviting sea
Almost an obnoxious bright blue
That swims in the mind

SOD

Do you have to be
Such a revolting sod whose mean
Words are so rotten

FALLING

Falling ever faster
Into a trap that fractures
Any semblance of logic

SEASON

Come my season of
Spring that sees nature's power
To grow red flowers

DRIVE

We went for a drive
Through the deep valley of ever
Green tall pine trees

FEAR

Call upon your steel
Eyed courage to face the fear
That you will not win

MAKE

To make something real
That hits the souls of so many
People who will need

APPLE

It is said that the
Apple does that not fall far from
The tree's twisted branch

MINIMUM

You said we could get
By with minimum effort
How wrong we were

POINT

Driving we soon paused
By an unexpected place
A new vantage point

NORMAL

She said that it is
Normal to feel hard anger
About being let down

FLUSHED

Standing at the edge
Of a high mountain snow fell
Feeling oh so cold

DAY

This day full of rain,
Thunder, lightening, and wind
Broken and burnt trees

MAGIC

What magic is this
That sends streams of red colours
Across the sunlit shore

TREASURE

I want you to have
This treasure I found deep
In my love struck heart

NATURE

Nature, I was told,
Never blows it by getting
The odd wrong colours

HORIZON

The far horizons so
Covered in the finest
Of grey swirling mists

SIMPLE

We thought it would be
So simple to let go of
Our love oh so deep

COURAGE

What courage this small
Seed has to ram through the dark,
Deep, hard, cold, wet soil

WONDER

I hope I will not
Loose the wonder I feel when
I see the sun rise

REACH

Reach for that final
Solution that will bring you
Your satisfaction

SHADOWS

Shadows of branches
Twisting on the bare dry ground
Waiting for hard rain

FREE

Oh to be free of
The trials of living life's wrong
Turns - to be so free

SPIRIT

I cannot feel the
Spirit of the wind that swirls
My windows are shut

TEARS

I want to know why
So many tears flow down your face
Speak and I will know

FALL

This year the tree's leaves
Hold steady against the cold
Be the last to fall

WHY

Why be oh so hard
On yourself when you know it
Can be put so right

LIGHT

Small clouds play with light
From the bright day's sunlight to
Make dancing patterns

STRIKE

The lightening strike
Brilliant light so blinding bright
Intense - hard rain falls

CAREFUL

Be ever careful
Protect yourself from bad words
That sting your true soul

DROP

The ancient vase with
Its impressive gold patterns
Please do not drop it

STONES

How old are these stones
Sitting in the fast river
Polished by water

SHARP

The lion's sharp eyes watch
The horizon with penetrating
Vision - the next kill

SUNRISE

Sitting on the high peak
In almost total darkness
Dawn's true light to come

EASY

It would be so easy
To forget why it happened
Yesterday has gone

AMAZING

Is it not amazing
That nature has a command
Over mixing colours

NEW

Every day is so new
When the sunrise awakens so
Many beautiful flowers

MOUNTAIN

The mountain stood in
The way of us reaching our
Goal - steep rocks falling

MEADOW

In the fresh green field
We fell fast asleep to dream
Meadows in the sun

LOVE

What love is this that
Fills our new fervent fresh days
With unending love

LIFE

There are times when life
Has become so tangled that
It breaks our reason

WINDOW

From the window we
Can see our trees growing fruit
To nourish our lives

GOOD

How good it is to
Feel the wind flush away our
Sorrow and dark thoughts

DESTINY

I would like to think
That destiny played its part
In finding our love

ANCIENT

In its ancient way
The yew tree so tall and strong
To thrive and prosper

PAPER

This crumpled piece of
Paper will be thrown into
The raging, fierce fire

ICE

Her ice cold stare felt
Like a bolt of anger till
His smile broke the mood

SAND

The sands of time run
So fast in the tall hour glass
Turn it over now

CRACK

The crack of thunder
So powerful that it shook
Us to the ground

TEAR

Please not shed a tear
We will meet again when the new
Year sheds its winter

LOST

They felt oh so lost
When they made a wrong turn on
The road to freedom

SIMPLE

Oh how I wish it
Could be simple to end the
Unending raw pain

TICKET

The ticket I hold
Oh so tight that I could not
Drop it to the ground

HUMAN

I am oh so sad
That I have to say that I
Am only human

ONLY

If only winter's bite
Is not so hard this new year
Harvest the reward

PALE

Today the dawn is
So pale without a hint of
A deep, rich, blue sky

HOPE

I do not want to
Reduce my ambitious dreams
To such a false hope

COMEDY

Tis a comedy of
Broken smiles when the old jokes
Fall on cold, deaf ears

WAIT

Every day I wake to
Wait to see if the new buds
Of spring have opened

FOREVER

The river rolls forever
Sending its fresh, cold, sparkling
Water to the sea

SAD

Would it not be sad
To lose the sense of nature's
Gift of our lives

AGE

When do we reach the
Age when we understand the
Sense of what we are

EXCUSE

What kind of excuse
Can you give to make me feel
I should not be angry

TREASURE

This treasure I feel
So deep within my heart knows
Only your true love

FREEDOM

Oh to have the freedom
To say what we want when our
Freedom is in peril

PERSON

Who is this person
That looks me dead in the eye to
Sneer at my presence

ESCAPE

Go on, go on, break
Away and escape the lion's
Hard savage hunger

HAT

Your funny hat that
Has too many clashing colours
Hides your deep soft eyes

STRAWBERRY

So red so full of
Seeds and juice that will flow
Bite down and enjoy

HARD

Why should it be so
Hard to break down a brick wall
That stand in our way

WELL

Be well my friend to
Shed what troubles your ageing
And painful bent body

HANG

Move it up and to
The right so my painting will
Hang on our white wall

LILLY

Oh how I wish that
Lilies would not remind us
Of death's undying night

OCEAN

I swim in the ocean
Of your love getting deeper
As the years flow past

DOG TOY

Ok young dog you killed
The squeak in your new toy but
Why did you bury it?

SPRING

It is just too full
Of wonder to witness the
Power of nature's spring

STEEL

With your steel eyed
Expression and your off words
Leave now - walk away

KING

The kind King spoke of
How he avoided war to keep
His people safe and free

SHARP

His answers were sharp
So much to the point that the
Teacher was speechless

HARBOUR

We sailed into
The harbour now safe from the
The boiling dark clouds

STORM

The storm on our hearts
Now calmed by feeling love's
Power to heal love

EDGE

The edge of the cliff
With its sharp stones and its long
Grass tickling our toes

FIRE

The fire burns so hot
That it sends plums of dark smoke
High into the night

SPRING

With each new warm day
Spring works nature's magic to
Bring fuel for our souls

BYGONE

Bygone days full of
Life's precious energy that
Flowes with such joy

WISE

They said that with old
Age wisdom grows to mellow
Our too hard emotions

ELECTRIC

We joined hands to
Make a circle - the teacher
Sent an electric shock

BROKEN

It lay broken on
The chair - to fix its smashed
Parts - really hard

ODD

How odd it will be
To return to a place that
Held only sorrow

PALACE

The palace stood on
The hill commanding the land
Such deep, dark, clouds, fell

BLACK

Leave your black mood
To come for a long walk with
Me and our two dogs

LEAF

The strange shaped leaf
Too exotic for our garden
Dropped by a bird

BOLD

Bold against the sky
A hawk flew in such sharp turns
Hunting its new prey

SHADOWS

In the shadows of
Grey ideas I have no place to
Clear them with cut words

BLUE

The sky is so blue
That it almost looks surreal
Clouds will cover it

WAKE

Please do not wake the
Hurt in me that feels so wrong
I am so sorry

FREEDOM

Give me the freedom
To love you with all my heart
Give it to only me

FLY

Fly with your crazy
Flight buzzing here buzzing there
Just sit on white wall

BUD

The bud so near to
Opening its rich red petals
Go winters's ice

ROSE

The rose opened its
Rich, dark, red, stunning petals
To welcome the sun